Can we win this game?

Too right we can win this game! We have a wicked team!

The players go onto the pitch.

The game begins. We play hard.

We soon get the ball and run fast. But can we keep it?

The ball stays with us, but it is hard to keep.

The team mark well. We dash for goal!

We can do it.

Boot the ball now! Hard and straight!

The pass is good.

We can go for goal ... **shoot now!!**
But can the goalie stop it?

At last the game is over. It's 1-0!

The fans chant and yell in the crowd! We did it! We won!